heart, mind & soul

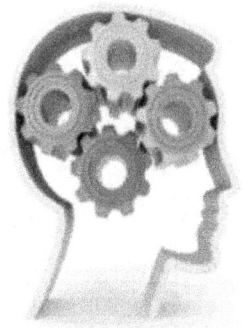

GWEN GIBBS

Heart, Mind & Soul

"An Assortment of Poetry"

By Gwen Gibbs

Cover Created by Jazzy Kitty Publications

Logo Designs by Andre M. Saunders/Jess Zimmerman

Images: Listed at the end of the book

Editor: Anelda Attaway

© 2020 Gwen Gibbs

ISBN 978-1-7357874-7-3

Library of Congress Control Number: 2020922659

All rights reserved. This book is protected by the copyright laws of the United States of America. This book may not be copied or reprinted for commercial gain or profit. The use of short quotations or occasional page copying for personal or group study is permitted and encouraged. Permission will be granted upon request. For Worldwide Distribution. Printed in the United States of America. Published by Jazzy Kitty Publications utilizing Microsoft Publishing Software and Bookcover Pro. The Holy Scriptures are from the Holy Bible.

ACKNOWLEDGMENTS

Giving honor and praise to God, the head of my life. Thank You, Lord, for placing this gift inside of me, and for trusting me to share with others the good news. Without You none of this would be possible.

DEDICATIONS

This book is dedicated to my wonderful husband Joe and our beautiful daughters Tiara and Tiyanna, I could not ask for a better family.

I would also like to say thanks to my awesome and gorgeous mother Ida Mason for being the best mother and friend a girl could ever have.

A special dedication to my wonderful and loving father the late Earl Mason Although you are no longer with us physically, you are always in Our Hearts, part of Our Soul and on Our Minds.

One love forever Pop

TABLE OF CONTENTS

INTRODUCTION……………………………………………...i

INSPIRATIONAL……………………………………………01

    Jesus Saves……………………………………………………03

    So Thankful……………………………………………………06

    He Chose Me…………………………………………………08

    The <u>J</u>ewel i<u>S</u> In <u>US</u> (JESUS)……………………………………10

    So Necessary…………………………………………………13

    When Under Attack…………………………………………15

    Peace in Your Soul…………………………………………18

    Rain On Us……………………………………………………22

    Angel in Disguise……………………………………………25

    Hang On………………………………………………………26

    Angel in Your Eyes…………………………………………29

    Know Your Place……………………………………………32

    Your Kiss from Heaven……………………………………35

    He is All………………………………………………………37

    Dream Chaser………………………………………………40

    Do You…………………………………………………………41

TABLE OF CONTENTS

    Live Life 42

    Nobody Can Be You But You 45

    What's Good 48

    My Story 52

    To New Beginnings 55

    God is Worthy of All Our Praise 56

ALL ABOUT LOVE 58

    Love Is 60

    Your Love 63

    This Love 66

    This Thing Called Love 68

    Can You Love Me? 69

    Essence of Your Love 72

    Magical Ways 74

    At First Glance 76

    Still of the Night 78

    Last Night I Dreamt 81

    Where Were You? 83

    Too Close 86

TABLE OF CONTENTS

    Pieces 88

    Walking Away 90

    Over You 94

    This Time Around 97

FOR AMUSEMENT **99**

    My Resolution 101

    White Christmas 103

    Puttin' on the Ritz 106

    First Date 108

    Queen for a Day 111

    Santa Clause 114

ALL-INCLUSIVE **117**

    Take a Little Trip 118

    Do You Remember? 122

    Family Way 124

    Blame it on the Moon 128

    Mask 130

    To Our Angels 133

    A Dream 136

TABLE OF CONTENTS

Dream Sleep...138

Who Are You?..140

A Mother's Love...143

Hello January...146

Spring Fever...149

Free...151

A Poets Worth..153

If Only..156

Angels Watching Over Me..158

Be Not Deceived..161

ABOUT THE AUTHOR..163

THE IMAGES...........…....................…..................164

INTRODUCTION

This is a book of an assortment of poetry. I feel that this book has something for everyone. It has inspiration if you are feeling low or need encouragement. If you are head over hills in love, I got you! If you feel like being a little silly, hopefully, I can make you smile. It has poems just for everyday life; I promise you can relate to at least one of the poems in this book.

So, come take a walk with me, hope you enjoy the journey.

INSPIRATIONAL

Gwen Gibbs

JESUS SAVES

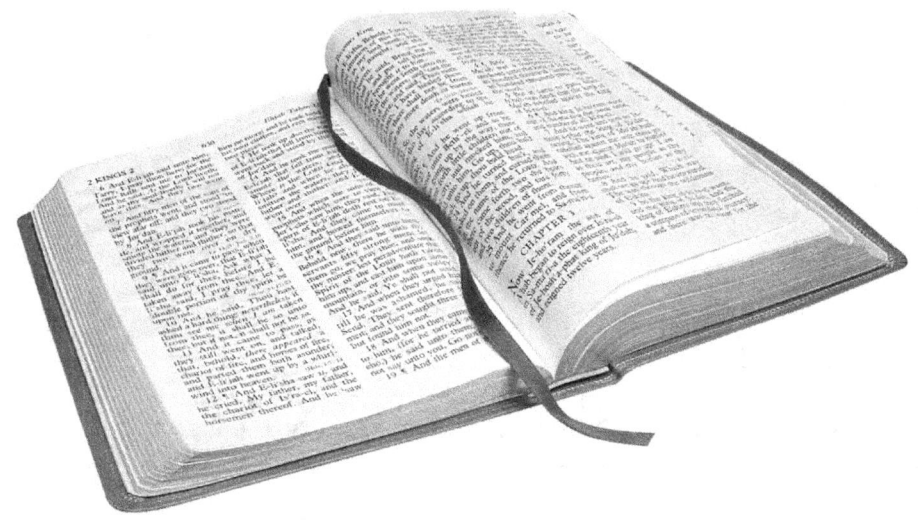

STAY IN GOD'S WORD

AND HE'LL KEEP YOU FROM FEAR

JESUS SAVES

Just in case you're

UNAWARE

Everything He gives us is because

He CARES

SO FREELY HE GAVE HIS SON

FOR OUR SIN

Unselfishly LOVING us

From Beginning to End

So many have come to know Him

As Father and Friend

Saved by His MERCY

And GRACE

All He wants is for us

To seek His Face

Gwen Gibbs

Vines stretch Forth and Fruits appear

Everyone who HEARS

Should have a Listening Ear

Stay in God's WORD

And He'll keep you from FEAR

SO THANKFUL

I AM SO THANKFUL

FOR THE JOY THAT I HAVE IN MY HEART

THAT ONLY GOD CAN GIVE

AND NO ONE CAN TEAR APART

SO THANKFUL

I am SO VERY THANKFUL

For Life and Health

Which means so much more than

GREAT WEALTH

I'VE HAD TRYING TIMES

I MUST ADMIT

But I thank God

For Bringing Me Through It

I am SO VERY THANKFUL

For Family and Friends

And for the Love and Laughter

That NEVER ENDS

For a shoulder to Lay My Head

Or a Listening Ear

And that Voice that Leaves me

WITHOUT any Fear

I am SO THANKFUL

For the Joy that I have in my Heart

That only God can give

And NO ONE Can Tear Apart

For His Grace and Mercy

Shown unto me

And for that I shall be

FOREVER INDEBTED to Thee

I am so Grateful

And Grateful I shall Forever Be

BECAUSE I KNOW THAT

JESUS DIED FOR ME

HE CHOSE ME

Lord, I Thank You

for CHOOSING ME

For Showing me EVERYTHING

That I Could Be

For Loving and Caring and Protecting me

And Keeping me from those things

That I Could Not See

Thank You Lord

For CHOOSING ME

For Trusting My Ability

To do what's Right

For Directing me in the Bright of Day

And Lighting My Path

In the Dark of Night

I thank you Lord

For CHOOSING ME

For You could have just

Let Me Be

Out in the World

WITHOUT a Clue

Not knowing that the Best Thing

For Me is You

Lord, I'm SO THANKFUL

For Your Peace and Grace

Which makes this Life MUCH EASIER

To Face

And now I know that since I have You

I don't have to Stay the Same

I can start out Fresh and New

THE JEWEL IS IN US

The Presence of the Lord
IS SO OVERWHELMING

It's like a PRECIOUS JEWEL
That sparkles brightly IN MY EYE
His Love comes in and Overtakes me
That all I can do is Cry

He Touches me so DEEPLY that words can
NEVER EXPLAIN
The Calming Presence that I Feel
WHEN I EARNESTLY CALL ON HIS NAME

He fills me with such Strength
And Stirs up a Fire within me
And all Glory, Honor and Praise is given unto Him
For WITHOUT His Guidance
Where would I be?

THE JEWEL IS JESUS

Who LIVES in our Hearts and Souls

He gets us through our Peaks and Valleys

And Pushes us to our Goals

For there is NO ONE Greater

In Heaven Or on Earth

Than JESUS CHRIST

Our Savior

Whom Showers us with LOVE

And IMMEASURABLE Favor

THE JEWEL IS IN US

Just continues to seek His face

AND EARNESTLY TRUST

SO NECESSARY

GOD LOVES US ALL SO VERY MUCH

THAT HE GAVE HIS ONLY SON

TO TAKE ON AND TO COVER

A MULTITUDE OF SIN FOR EVERYONE

SO NECESSARY

God is SO NECESSARY

In EVERYTHING we do

For by Him you were Created

And He knows what's Best for you

I'd hate to see Where we Would be

Without His Love and Grace

We'd probably NEVER walk around

With a SMILE upon our Face

God Loves us ALL So Very Much

That He gave His ONLY SON

To take On and to Cover a Multitude of Sin

FOR EVERYONE

God could have TURNED His Back on Us

And Frowned with Disgrace

But yet, He chose to FORGIVE US

Despite our Faults on a Daily Base

What an AWESOME GOD

We are Blessed to be Serving

He ALWAYS looks out for us

Even though we're NOT Deserving

NO ONE ELSE could Always be there

And Care for us so much

So we should ALWAYS have Faith in Him

AND IN GOD SHALL WE TRUST

WHEN UNDER ATTACK

When you're UNDER ATTACK

You have to WATCH YOUR BACK

Don't lose Focus of your Surrounding

You MUST Stay On Track

Keep your Sight Stable and your Head Level

And stay Girded Up

And ready to FIGHT that devil

Some Situations in Life

Can really throw you for a Loop

And if you're NOT CAREFUL

It will Show you how Low you can Stoop

With things in Life

You must Learn how to Cope

And Continue to Empower your mind

So you DON'T Lose Hope

There's Power in the Tongue

So Speak GOOD OVER YOURSELF

Instead of Feeling Despair

Think thoughts of Great Wealth

God equipped you with a Powerful Mind

So let it Work for you

If you use it as it was Intended

His Grace will see you through

When UNDER ATTACK

Don't look Back, look Ahead

And stay in God's Word

So your Soul Can Be Fed

You'll find Strength

To keep you Standing Tall

And with God on your side

You can Scale that WALL

PEACE IN YOUR SOUL

FORGIVENESS IS THE KEY

TO A HEALTHY LIVING

WE STRUGGLE WITH AN UNHAPPY SOUL

IF WE HARBOR UNFORGIVING

PEACE IN YOUR SOUL

There's NOTHING like PEACE

In the Midst of a Storm

It's like a Blanket on a Cold Day

To help keep us Warm

When your Soul and Mind

Are in PERFECT PEACE

It gives us a Feeling

Of Such A Great Release

Like Floating on a Soft Cloud

Up in the Sky Above

The PEACE ONLY God gives

Because of His

UNCONDITIONAL LOVE

Without the LORD'S PEACE

We would all be Lost

So we thank Him for the PEACE

He gives WITHOUT Cost

We can't have PEACE

If we Hold On to a Lifelong Grudge

Because it Keeps us from Growing

And being OPEN TO LOVE

FORGIVENESS is the Key

To a Healthy Living

We Struggle with an unhappy Soul

If we harbor Unforgiving

Regardless of what the other person has done

We must FORGIVE and LET GO

In order for our Battle to be Won

Be in Control of your own Destiny

Be determined to be SET FREE

Live a Happy and Healthy Life

And keep yourself from Pain and Strife

Heart, Mind & Soul

RAIN ON US

RAIN ON US LORD

AND SEND DOWN YOUR BLESSING

HELP US FIGURE OUT

THE THINGS IN OUR LIVES

THAT NEED ADDRESSING

RAIN ON US

RAIN ON US LORD

And Send Down Your BLESSING

Help us Figure out

The Things in our Lives

That Need Addressing

Let Your LIGHT

So Brightly Shine

And with a Firm Hand

KEEP US IN LINE

So that we WON'T Lose Sight

Of who we are

We will Keep our Eyes fixed

On that Northern Star

Without You Lord

There would be ONLY Dark Days

The whole world would Walk Around

IN A CONSTANT HAZE

But You Oh Lord

ARE THE LIGHT OF THE WORLD

And Shall Forever Be

The ONLY ONE that can truly Set

Our Souls Free

SO RAIN ON US Oh Lord

And Shower us with Your Love

We'll always know our Source of Strength

COMES FROM ABOVE

ANGEL IN DISGUISE

ANGELS ARE ALL AROUND US

BRINGING SAFETY TO OUR GAME

AND KEEPING US COVERED EVERY DAY

BUT WE DON'T KNOW THEIR NAME

ANGEL IN DISGUISE

ANGELS come IN ALL DISGUISES

Be it Big or Small

Continue to keep your Spiritual Eyes Open

And watch ON WHOM you Call

Cause ANGELS are ALL AROUND US

Bringing Safety to our Game

And keeping us Covered Every Day

But we don't know their Name

Care about and Love those around you

And to EACH ONE be Kind

Because you NEVER know who you're Entertaining

Behind the DISGUISE

AN ANGEL YOU JUST MIGHT FIND

HANG ON

When Life hands you a Heavy Load

And your left Feeling like

A Warted Toad

You've been Knocked Down

Flat on your Back

And feel that you are

UNDER GREAT ATTACK

Things start to Mess with your Mind

The longer you Dwell on it

You get Further Behind

You feel that Now

You've COME to the Very End

Not realizing that all you have to Do is

BEGIN AGAIN

Starting Over Again

Can be a BIG CHALLENGE at First

But staying in a Downtrodden State

Can Be Even Worse

You are much Greater than

You choose to S<small>EE</small>

So Stand up STRONG

And Become what you were MEANT TO BE

Yes, HARD TIMES will Come

But you must HOLD ON

The more you Work Through It

The SOONER it'll be Gone

There's been a PURPOSE for your Life

Since the Day you were Born

SO VISUALIZE THAT AND BE STRONG

Don't let the NEGATIVE

Keep you Torn

From Dusk to Dawn

As Night Turns to Morn

NEVER GIVE UP

JUST HANG ON

ANGEL IN YOUR EYES

You look up to the Sky and it is No Surprise

The beauty that you see

IS AN ANGEL IN YOUR EYES

It NEVER Fails that

When you're Down and Feeling Blue

THE ANGEL IN YOUR EYES

Is Sitting Watching Over You

In all the Hustle and Bustle of your day

And Oh How Time Flies

But in the Midst of it all

There sits that ANGEL IN YOUR EYES

Just staying close to Guide you

Along a Dusty Road

And there to Help you Carry

Some of Life's Heavy Load

You thank the Lord above

Each Day that you ARISE

Yet are so Unaware

That there's an

ANGEL IN YOUR EYES

KNOW YOUR PLACE

STAND UP STRONG AND TALL

AND RUN A GOOD RACE

AND IT DOESN'T EVEN MATTER

IF YOU DON'T COME IN FIRST PLACE

BELIEVE IN WHO YOU ARE

AND KNOW THAT YOU ARE A WINNER

KNOW YOUR PLACE

It's Important to

KNOW YOUR PLACE

In this Time and Space

Don't look Down, look Up

At the Obstacle you Face

Stand up Strong and Tall

And Run a GOOD RACE

And it doesn't even matter

If you DON'T Come in First Place

Believe in who you are

And know that YOU ARE A WINNER

Like the Roadrunner who Refuses to be

Anyone's Dinner

Keep On Moving

And let NOTHING Pull you Back

BE PERSISTENT

And stay on the Right Side of the Track

Keep your Head up to the Sky

And let the Light EMBRACE you

Be Confident in what you do

And to thine own self be True

It all comes down to

What you Choose to make of it

So make sure that

YOU KNOW YOUR PLACE

AND NEVER EVER QUIT

A KISS FROM HEAVEN

YOUR KISS FROM HEAVEN

IS SO UNLIKE ANY OTHER

IT'S SORT OF LIKE A KISS

A CHILD WOULD GET FROM

A MOTHER

YOUR KISS FROM HEAVEN

YOUR KISS FROM HEAVEN

Is so UNLIKE any other

It's Sort of like a Kiss

A Child would get From

A Mother

With such Soft Sweet Tenderness

At Hand

And on the Perfect Spot

On the Cheek it would Land

YOUR KISS FROM HEAVEN

Is much like a Wonderful Dream

Like Floating in the Summer

On a raft Downstream

While the Sun warms your Body

With its Glow

The Happiness that you Feel

Just can't help but Show

YOUR KISS FROM HEAVEN

Can sometimes be Intense

You try to figure it out

But it just doesn't make Sense

You come to the Conclusion

That it was just meant to be

And that this Kiss you have Received

IS YOUR REALITY

HE IS ALL

We were UNIQUELY Made

By the HANDS of a Pro

With a Single Breath of Air

To set us on the Go

Like a man Controls a Puppet

We could have been

But instead, He gave FREE WILL

To all Women and Men

The WILL to Choose

And to Do

WHATEVER WE PLEASE

With the Hopes that we would Remember

OUR MAKER

And Bow Down on our Knees

He could have Directed our Move

In every way

But decided to allow us to go about on our own

From Day to Day

It is not by our Will that we Continue

To get by

But by His HEAVENLY HAND

That Leads us from the Sky

REVERENCE THE LORD

With all of your Might

Because after all

He is the Day and Night

DREAM CHASER

CHASE A DREAM

Until you Find it

NEVER give up on you

For if you STOP SHORT of your Quest

You'll never get

WHAT YOU WERE DUE

DO YOU

Be the Best at what you Do

And ALWAYS Stay On Top

Don't get Distracted on your Path

And let your Vision Pop

Be Diligent and Go Forth

With all your Power and Might

And whatever it is your going for

Keep right there in Sight

Be the Best at what you Do

And don't be a Copycat

JUST DO YOU

LIVE LIFE

Trust in your Instincts

And Believe in you

GIVE 100 PERCENT

To EVERYTHING you Pursue

LIVE LIFE

LIVE LIFE to the Fullest

And DON'T Look Back

Keep a Level Head and Stay On Track

Know where you're Going

And REACH for your Goal

Keep On Believing

Deep Down in your Soul

Go One Step Above

What you normally do

Never stop trying until

YOU SEE IT THROUGH

Trust in your Instincts and believe in you

GIVE 100 PERCENT

To EVERYTHING you Pursue

In the End you will feel Proud

SO STAND UP STRONG

And Laugh Out Loud

Always know you've done your Best

And find New Things

To take you on a Quest

NOBODY CAN BE YOU BUT YOU

Take a look in the Mirror

And what do you see?

You see the Unique Person

God made you to be

He took His time and Made you well

And in this Process

He COULD NOT Fail

He made you with Love

And Care in His Heart

And was Oh So Pleased with

His Created Work of Art

He made you so very Different

From all of the Rest

And that is why you are daily Tried

And put to the Test

But He placed such STRENGTH inside of you

So you can Endure

The Snares and Glares that come

WON'T PENETRATE ANYMORE

So look Inside yourself and See the Person

That you've Grown into

Search Deep Down in your Heart

And to yourself be True

And Always Remember

THAT NOBODY CAN BE YOU BUT YOU

WHAT'S GOOD?

STRENGTHENING YOUR MIND AND SOUL

SO ON TRACK YOU WILL STAY

KNEELING DOWN EACH

DAY AND NIGHT

TO THANK GOD AS YOU PRAY

WHAT'S GOOD?

Life is GOOD if you make it that way

Seeking out the Sunshine

Through Skies of Grey

Keeping a Positive Attitude

On a regular Day to Day

Never letting the Blues

Make your Joy Fade Away

Knowing and Believing that you can do

What you set out to

Pressing Forward and Continually Striving

Until you see it through

Strengthening your Mind and Soul

So On Track you will stay

Kneeling Down EACH Day and Night

To thank God as you PRAY

Learning from the Lessons

That Life has TAUGHT you

Always keeping it Real

And Searching to keep things NEW

Being yourself

Not letting people CHANGE who you are

Believing in yourself

And being the BEST YOU by far

Keep a Level Head

And REMEMBER what Mamma said

Always Be Open to New Things

And ALLOW yourself to be Fed

Remember to Always keep

An ATTAINABLE Goal before you

So that you will have Something

To look Forward to

WHAT'S GOOD today is

Whatever you Choose to make it

Life, Love, Health and Happiness

Could all be yours JUST TAKE IT

Be kind, Compassionate and Caring

To one another

Be it Stranger, Friend, Mother,

Father, Sister Or Brother

Just know in your Heart

That at the End of the Day

You're able to say

I did EVERYTHING in My Ability

TO MAKE A DIFFERENCE TODAY

MY STORY

MY STORY IS SIMPLE

AND PLAN TO BE TOLD

I'LL ALWAYS CHOOSE JESUS

OVER SILVER AND GOLD

MY STORY

MY STORY is not one of

Overnight Sensation

It isn't even one that would get

A Standing Ovation

No Crowd Cheering for another Encore

No Limos or Screaming Fans

Outside the door

MY STORY is not one of

Great Success Achieved

If I told you it was so you

Would TRULY be Deceived

No Mountain of Cash

Storing up in the Bank

Sometimes NOT EVEN enough Fuel

In My Gas Tank

MY STORY is truly one of

Faith and Trust in God

This journey I travel to some

May seem Quite Odd

But it is through my Faith

That I find Strength on a Daily Base

And am able to Ignore the Penetrating Looks

On People's Face

MY STORY is Trust that God is with me

Wherever I may go

And He tells me I'm SPECIAL to Him

And this I'll ALWAYS know

Don't need to be a Star On Earth

Because I am in His EYES

No need for Ego Boosters

Because God keeps me on the Rise

MY STORY is Simple

And Plan to be Told

I'll always CHOOSE JESUS

Over Silver and Gold

I'd rather have Something

That's truly Guaranteed

Instead of something achieved

Purely through Greed

TO NEW BEGINNINGS

Here's Looking Forward

TO NEW BEGINNINGS

With Good Things Ahead

And Happy Endings

No more LOOKING BACK

And Dwelling on the Past

Let's work toward something that's going to Last

Reach for the Stars and Touch the Sky

Don't Drag on the Bottom

Try Flying High

Jump out and Test your Flight

For DESTINY

And take a Breath and See

How Freeing it can be

Know the Greatness

That Dwells INSIDE OF YOU

And be very Confident of the things

You Can Do

The Light in you

CANNOT be Hid Away

It must SHINE Brighter

And Brighter every day

So here's looking

TO NEW BEGINNINGS

Let's all do our Best

To make this Year one

THAT SHALL TRULY BE BLESSED

GOD IS WORTHY OF ALL OUR PRAISE

GOD IS WORTHY OF ALL OUR PRAISE

He carries us through all our days

He clears our minds when in a haze

And leads us through this crazy maze

GOD IS WORTHY OF ALL OUR PRAISE

When you were supposed to be shot

it was only a graze

And you thought you were losing your mind

But it was only a faze

So why wouldn't you praise Him

In all His ways

GOD IS WORTHY OF ALL OF OUR PRAISING

You walked out alive

when the house was blazing

You made it through the hard times

you were facing

Our God is just truly and simply

AMAZING

Gwen Gibbs

ALL ABOUT LOVE

LOVE IS

LOVE IS

A FEELING

FROM DEEP WITHIN

LOVE IS

MORE THAN A BOND

BETWEEN A FRIEND

Gwen Gibbs

LOVE IS

LOVE IS

A Feeling

From Deep Within

LOVE IS

More than a Bond

Between a Friend

LOVE

Can be Warm and Satisfying

LOVE

Can be Painful

And Leave you Crying

LOVE

Comes from many Places

LOVE

Shows on Different Faces

LOVE IS

Colorful and Bright

LOVE IS

In the Stars at Night

LOVE IS

The Man You Marry

LOVE IS

The Baby You Carry

LOVE

Should have

No Pain or Sorrow

LOVE

should have only

A Brighter Tomorrow

So LOVE

The one you're with

And NEVER be Untrue

For if you Stoop to this

Your Heart will forever be Blue

YOUR LOVE

YOUR LOVE

Is like the Wind Blowing

Through my hair

YOUR LOVE

Is like a Child Born

Without a Care

YOUR LOVE

Is like your Face

So Sensitive yet Strong

YOUR LOVE

Is what I'm Hoping for

TO LAST MY WHOLE LIFE LONG

YOUR LOVE

Is like the Sea Rushing

To the Shore

YOUR LOVE

Is what I need More and More

YOUR LOVE

Can make me Laugh

YOUR LOVE

Can make me Cry

YOUR LOVE

Makes me NEVER

Want to say Goodbye

These things Come from the Heart

And they need NEVER part

I'll always think Strongly of

YOUR PRECIOUS LOVE

THIS LOVE I FEEL

THIS LOVE I FEEL

IS SO SURREAL

IT'S SOMETHING THAT I THOUGHT

I'D NEVER FEEL

THIS LOVE I FEEL

THIS LOVE I FEEL

Is so Surreal

It's something that I thought

I'd NEVER feel

Like Blowing through the Wind

On a Starry Night

Or knowing that you're Wrong

But FEELING Oh So Right

THIS LOVE I FEEL

Is sometimes Confusing

I know I'm Winning

But I feel like I'm Losing

I think that my FEELINGS are True

But the more I ponder it

I begin FEELING BLUE

Could THIS LOVE be Something

That's meant to be

Or am I trying Too Hard

To make it the

PERFECT FAIRYTALE for me

Could it be Something

That I've Just Made up in my Head

Or is my HEART STARVING so much

And Waiting to be Fed

THIS THING CALLED LOVE

What is THIS THING CALLED LOVE

Is it being served Breakfast in Bed

Or is it Waking up Reminiscing

About the Sweet Words he said

What is THIS THING CALLED LOVE

Is it he Loves me, he Loves me NOT

Or could it be that I've FINALLY REALIZED

What I've Got

Love is a Powerful Thing

Emotions Run Wild

As it TUGS at your Heart String

To be in Love is REALLY Great

But don't just Settle for any Old Date

For when it is RIGHT the Sparks will Light

Cause THIS THING CALLED LOVE is Dynomite

CAN YOU LOVE ME?

CAN YOU LOVE ME

For who I am?

CAN YOU LOVE ME

For where I Stand?

CAN YOU LOVE ME

In Spite of my Faults?

CAN YOU LOVE ME

Without throwing Sharp Darts?

CAN YOU LOVE ME

In Sickness and in Health?

CAN YOU LOVE ME

Without Great Wealth?

CAN YOU LOVE ME

When Times get Tough?

CAN YOU LOVE ME

When the Road gets Rough?

CAN YOU LOVE ME

When I'm being Mean?

CAN YOU LOVE ME

When the Grass is no longer Green

CAN YOU LOVE ME

Without looking at my past?

CAN YOU LOVE ME

And Make our Love Last?

If you CAN LOVE ME

In all of these ways

Your Love is known to be Unconditional

AND THAT IS REAL LOVE

ESSENCE OF YOUR LOVE

OH, THE ESSENCE OF YOUR LOVE

GOES SO FAR ABOVE

CAUSE WHAT I'VE FOUND IN YOU

HAS GOT TO BE LOVE

ESSENCE OF YOUR LOVE

Our Love was SO NEW

When First we met

Day turned to night

And with the Night was NO REGRETS

The Soft Caress of your Hand

Against My Skin

Your Lips pressed against mine

Pulling me in

The Sweet Sultry looks

That you give to me

Seems to set My Body and Soul Free

You're constantly taking me

To Higher Heights

As night turns to Day

And days turn to Nights

My Head is in a Spin

With this LOVE AFFAIR I'm in

Whatever Game we're Playing

I'll come up with the Win

OH, THE ESSENCE OF YOUR LOVE

Goes so far Above

Cause what I've found in you

Has Got to Be LOVE

MAGICAL WAYS

The way you Do

The things you Do

The Words you say that Sound So True

You make me Feel So Alive

You Brighten up a Dark Room

When you come inside

It must be your MAGICAL WAYS

You're the Life of the Party

You fill everyone with Joy

You're so Playful sometimes

You remind me of a Little Boy

You're the Happiest person I know

That's why I Love You So

You make me Smile for Days

It must be your MAGICAL WAYS

I CAN'T FIGURE OUT

How you do it Every Day of your Life

The World of Today is in such Distress

But yet and still

You are NEVER Depressed

You STAND Strong and Tall

With a Smile that Shines On All

You bring us Love from your Heart

And as I said from the Start

It must be your MAGICAL WAYS

AT FIRST GLANCE

AT FIRST GLANCE

I thought I had a Chance

Thought what we had was

TRUE ROMANCE

Until you gave me

The old Song and Dance

But at least you gave me Notice

IN ADVANCE

I was Mesmerized

By your Flair and Style

My head was in a Whirlwind

For a while

Up on Cloud Nine

is where I once Landed

Until you Brought Me Down

And left me Empty Handed

My Feet DIDN'T Touch the Ground

Whenever you were Around

I'd look Deep into your Eyes

But couldn't make a Sound

No Words Could Express

The Love that I thought I had Found

When the WHOLE TIME I Never Knew

That I was being CLOWNED

AT FIRST GLANCE

It looked so much Different to me

But at last now my Eyes are Open

And have Come to See

And I'm SO THANKFUL to You

For SETTING ME FREE

Because You and I were NEVER Really

MEANT TO BE

STILL OF THE NIGHT

IN THE STILL OF THE NIGHT

Where the Moon is Shining Bright

Our Imagination takes Flight

As the Star gives way to Light

IN THE STILL OF THE NIGHT

As we Gaze out into the Big Blue Sky

Tears of Joy start to fill my Eyes

As I take a Breath and give a Great Sigh

IN THE STILL OF THE NIGHT

Feelings of Love

Start to Flow

Overflow of Emotions start

To Grow

And where this WILL END

ONLY YOU AND I KNOW

THE STILL OF THE NIGHT

Can take us Places Unknown

Sending us Shivering with Chills

Down to the Bone

PLEASURABLE GRATIFICATION

That Incites me to a Moan

And the Evening is ours

In which to Set the Tone

LAST NIGHT I DREAMT

I DREAMT THAT YOU

CALLED TO ME AND SAID

YOU'D SOON BE HERE

BUT WHEN I OPENED MY EYES

I FOUND YOU WERE NOWHERE NEAR

LAST NIGHT I DREAMT

LAST NIGHT I DREAMT

That you were Here with me

Just a Kiss AWAY

From Sweet Serenity

I DREAMT

That you and I would soon be Wed

But when I Awoke

It was just me alone in my Bed

I DREAMT that you

Called to me and said

You'd SOON be Here

But when I Opened My Eyes

I found you were NOWHERE Near

Since realizing that it was

ONLY A DREAM

I'm now wondering how

Reality would Seem

WHERE WERE YOU?

WHERE WERE YOU?

When I NEEDED you the Most

When I Cried out your Name

You disappeared like a Ghost

WHERE WERE YOU?

When I needed your Help in the Dark of Night

Just a Moment Ago you were by my Side

And now you're Out of Sight

You PROMISED that you would be Here

To keep me Safe From Harm

And Hold Me Tight and Closely

In the Comfort of your Arms

To help me Find My Way

When I get Lost

And shelter me at ALL COST

It wouldn't be So Bad for Me

If you hadn't GIVEN me False Hope

Because Once Upon a Time in my Life

I COULD COPE

I guess I Trusted and Depended on you

TOO MUCH

And in the End

All you Handed me was just a Crutch

So now I must Learn Once Again

To get along WITHOUT you

And get myself up Off the Ground

And start off FRESH and NEW

Dust off and Get up and Go

What's ahead for me

I DON'T KNOW

You could have told me Something

Instead of leaving me Sad and Blue

The only question unanswered for me is

WHERE WERE YOU?

TOO CLOSE

You're getting TOO CLOSE to me

That I can Hardly See

I want to be with you

But I need Room to be Free

I like the Time we spend Together

And Enjoy your Company

But whenever we're Together

I feel you're Overwhelming me

You're getting TOO CLOSE to me

That I can Barely Breath

And when I Try to Walk Away

You Hold on to my Sleeve

I only need a Little Space

To put my Mind at Ease

But when I Try to Slip Away

You Grab on to my Knees

You're getting TOO CLOSE to me

That I can't Think ANY MORE

So Badly, I just want to go Running

For the Door

The Time we Spend Together is

Just TOO MUCH time Indeed

It seems to me the Problem is

That you're just to IN NEED

PIECES

I'm Falling to PIECES

And I don't know why

Sometimes I feel So Low

That I just Sit and Cry

I want SO BADLY to get up

But something's Weighing Me Down

I try so Hard to Force a Smile

But all I can do is Frown

I'm Falling to PIECES

And I can't get it together

Sometimes I feel my Life is full of

Grey and Stormy Weather

It's tough to keep my Head to the Sky

When Each and Every Day

I STRUGGLE TO GET BY

My Life might be in

LITTLE BITTY PIECES RIGHT NOW

But PIECE BY PIECE

I'm gonna Turn this Thing Around

WALKING AWAY

I'M WALKING AWAY

From this Affair

It's Funny but it seems

You Just Don't Care

About the Way

That I feel Inside

I'M SORRY BUT

I just CANNOT Hide

How VERY BADLY

You have Hurt me

I know you are Blind

And Cannot See

But it's ABOUT TIME

I Opened up My Eyes

And put a Halt to all those Nightly Cries

I'M WALKING AWAY

From this Affair

Of the Pain you have Caused me

You are Unaware

You want Me to Stand by you

And Keep my Mouth Shut

And Cater to your Every

Whim NO MATTER what

Now EVERY TIME I see you

It's like a Punch to the Gut

Which only lets me know

How DEEPLY I've Been Cut

So Goodbye to this Affair

Maybe now you'll Care

When you Turn Around

And I'm NO LONGER there

That is the Consequence

That you MUST Bare

OVER YOU

NO NEED TO CHANGE THE LOCKS

ON THE DOOR

CAUSE I WON'T BE

COMING BACK AROUND

OVER YOU

When we FIRST Got Together

Everything was just GREAT

But here Lately with Every Move

We seem to Hesitate

If I wanna go Left

You wanna go Right

And EVERY SINGLE DAY we just

Fight, Fight, Fight

Can't IMAGINE us ever

Getting along like we used to

Cause it seems that as

Time goes by I'm just SIMPLY OVER YOU

We Don't TALK ANYMORE

We just YELL at Each Other

We SNEAK and TIPTOE around the House

Like were Undercover

And it seems as though I've come to be

Your PAST TIME LOVER

I guess you THINK that after you

I COULD NEVER FIND ANOTHER

The way we're Living now, JUST WON'T DO

Cause at this Point and Time

I'M JUST SIMPLY OVER YOU

When I leave

DON'T come Looking for Me

Cause I don't WANNA be Found

No need to Change the Locks

ON THE DOOR

Cause I won't be

Coming Back Around

Life with you has just left me

Feeling Blue

And Quite Frankly

I'm certain that

I'M JUST SIMPLY OVER YOU

THIS TIME AROUND

THIS TIME AROUND

Won't be like the Rest

I'm gonna take my time

AND DO WHAT'S BEST

Reach for the Stars and Touch the Sky

Soar with the Wind Beneath My Wings and Fly

THIS TIME AROUND

Won't be Touch and Go

Because I KNOW what I Like

And I like what I Know

I am Smart and I'm Strong

And I know my Worth

And will Stand Out

And be Counted on this Earth

THIS TIME AROUND

Will be up Instead of Down

No long Twisty Turns

Or Slow Sinking Ground

Because this Lost Person

Has NOW been found

And I REFUSE to Remain Captive

And Be Bound

THIS TIME AROUND

I'm GONNA make it Through

Gonna do all the things I know I should do

Fight a GOOD FIGHT

All the way to the END

Go for what I know

AND ON MYSELF DEPEND

FOR AMUSEMENT

MY RESOLUTION

WORK HARD AT GETTING HEALTHY AND FIT

AND A COUPLE OF MONTHS WILL SHOW

IF I MADE IT

THAT'S MY RESOLUTION FOR 2021

TO PLAIN

AND SIMPLY GET IT DONE

MY RESOLUTION

A New Year a New you

That's what I Plan to do

To get this Body Back on Track

And Possibly work towards a Six Pack

Work Hard at getting Healthy and Fit

And a Couple of Months will SHOW

IF I MADE IT

That's MY RESOLUTION for 2021

To Plain

And Simply get it Done

WHITE CHRISTMAS

I'M DREAMING OF

A WHITE CHRISTMAS

WITH THE SNOW LAYING ON TOP

OF THE ROOF

AND THE SOUND OF

SANTA'S REINDEERS HOOF

WHITE CHRISTMAS

I'm Dreaming of

A WHITE CHRISTMAS

With the snow laying on Top of the Roof

And the sound of Santa's Reindeers Hoof

As they make their Rounds

Throughout the Town

It Rings out such a Joyful Sound

A WHITE CHRISTMAS

Would be So Lovely and Bright

It gives you the Feeling that Dreams

Still take Flight

Oh what a WONDERFUL SIGHT it would be

To have a WHITE CHRISTMAS

Around My Tree

I'm Dreaming of

A WHITE CHRISTMAS

And the Snowman I'll make

And afterwards we'll settle in

And take a Coffee Break

OH CHRISTMAS

OH CHRISTMAS

Please Paint the Canvas White

And create a Winter Wonderland

WHILE I'M ASLEEP TONIGHT

PUTTIN' ON THE RITZ

DANCING UP A STORM

TO ALL THE LATEST HITS

NOW THAT'S WHAT'S KNOWN

AS PUTTIN' ON THE RITZ

PUTTIN' ON THE RITZ

The Highest of the Class

With lots of Flowing Cash

With Gorgeous Evening Ball Gowns

And Tuxes with the Sash

They come to Drink

And Dance the Night Away

And NO ONE goes Home Till

They see the Light of Day

The Expensive Luxurious Cars

That Come and Go

Traveling Miles from a Distance

To get to the Show

The men Watch and Admire

The women on the Sly

As the Ladies Sashay across the Room

To catch a Wondering Eye

The Horns start to Blowing

And the Base gets to Bumping

And Shortly after that this Joint Starts

To Jumping

The men grab the Ladies Hands

And Lead them to the Stage

And before you know it

Everyone's Dancing up the Latest Rage

The Ladies Stay Cute

And the Men Stay Cool

Never Lose your Cool

That's the Golden Rule

Dancing up a Storm

To all the Latest Hits

Now that's what's Known

AS PUTTIN' ON THE RITZ

FIRST DATE

Our FIRST DATE

Didn't TURN OUT So Great

You were so Close to Me

That I couldn't Concentrate

I told you that I didn't want

To be out Too Late

So you took me to McDonalds

FOR A CHEAP DINNER DATE

You had the Nerve to call The Next Day

And ask me if EVERYTHING

Was Fine?

When you took me out

For a Burger and Soda

Instead of a nice Steak

And a Glass of Wine

I couldn't help but Lash out at you

Because you Ruined My Night

Then thought when you got Home

That EVERYTHING was Alright

So Please LOSE my number

And Stay out of My Sight

Because if I ever see you again

We just might have to Fight

QUEEN FOR A DAY

IF I WERE QUEEN FOR A DAY

I WOULD SIT ON MY THROWN

LOVING MYSELF AND EVERYTHING I OWN

QUEEN FOR A DAY

If I were QUEEN FOR A DAY

I would SIT on My Thrown

Loving myself and Everything I own

Being Pampered from Head to Toe

Traveling WORLDWIDE

Where ever I Want to Go

If I were QUEEN FOR A DAY

I would Live in a Castle

Living the Life of Glamour Free

From ALL HASSLE

Relaxing on a Secluded Beach

In the Bahamas

And Sipping Endlessly

On Bahama Mamas

If I were QUEEN FOR A DAY

I would Dress to the Nine

Everything I WEAR would have me

Looking So Fine

Smelling of Perfume that's

Oh So Sweet

Living in the Lap of Luxury

Just can't be Beat

All Hail to the QUEEN

Which is Me

Be it Real or Fantasy

But wouldn't it be Great to See

A Dream become a Reality

SANTA CLAUSE

There once was a Man

With a Long White Beard

And people Looked at Him as though

He were Weird

SANTA CLAUSE

There once was a Man

With a Long White Beard

And people Looked at Him as though

He were Weird

He wore a Big Red Suit

All Around Town

But was Oh So Happy

For NO ONE could bring him Down

He Traveled all across

The sea worldwide

With his Faithful Sidekick

Rudolph by his Side

His Goal for the Day

Was to Stock up Lots of Toys

And Deliver them to

All the Good Little Girls and Boys

With his Red Suit, Sleigh, and Reindeer

He Started out into the Night

Without ANY Fear

Through the Rain, Sleet, Snow

And Hail

He'd reach his Destination

Without Fail

He'd flop down each Chimney

With Grace

And Imagine the Beautiful Smiles

ON EACH CHILD'S FACE

When they Woke up

And saw their Surprise

The thought of it

Brought Tears to His Eyes

As he Dashed Off in

And out of each House

Without a Pause

His name you ask me?

Well of course, it's

SANTA CLAUSE

ALL-INCLUSIVE

TAKE A LITTLE TRIP

TAKE A LITTLE TRIP

Through your Mind and Explore it

Dive Deep into your Thoughts

Don't Ignore it

Check out what really Drives you

What do you really Go

Through when you are Happy

And when you are Blue

How do you Decide

The NEXT STEP to Take

Or determine between what's Real

And what's Fake

Dive Deeper and Find out

What makes you Mad

Check the Inner Parts

And find out what's Good and Bad

TAKE A LITTLE TRIP

Through your Mind and Explore it

Dissect each and every part

BIT BY BIT

Find out what Makes you Strong

And what Makes you Weak

Search the Inner Thoughts of your Mind

Don't play Hide and Seek

Break through those Barriers

That Hold you Down

No Longer shall you Allow them

To keep you Bound

Tap into your Strengths and Power

Envision yourself up

On the Highest Tower

Step out and Soar

On the Wings of the Wind

Everything that you Need to Make it

Comes from Within

Guide all your Thoughts,

Dreams and Hopes

And with Life

YOU WILL BE ABLE TO COPE

Be ALL that you Can be

And DO NOT STRAY

Keep a Level Head

And EVERYTHING will be Ok

TAKE A LITTLE TRIP

Through Your Mind Today

DO YOU REMEMBER

DO YOU REMEMBER

WHEN BREAD WAS JUST A NICKEL

AND YOU WEREN'T ALWAYS LEFT BROKE

AND IN A PICKLE

DO YOU REMEMBER?

DO YOU REMEMBER?

Back in the Good Old Days

When you would Lay in the Grass

And Look at the Sky in Amaze

DO YOU REMEMBER?

When Bread was just a Nickel

And you weren't always Left Broke

And in a Pickle

DO YOU REMEMBER?

Leaving your Door UNLOCKED

And No One Cared

But Now Days you CAN'T do that

Because you're TOO SCARED

DO YOU REMEMBER?

Going to the Store for Candy with just a Dime

But now to buy Candy from the Store

You must work Overtime

DO YOU REMEMBER?

When neighbors would Look Out

For Each Other

But today that doesn't happen Unless

You are a Sister or Brother

DO YOU REMEMBER?

When all you had to do is your very best

But now EVERYTHING is a Challenge

And we're always Put to a Test

DO YOU REMEMBER?

FAMILY WAY

The Special People in my Life

There with me through Struggles and Strife

A shoulder to Cry On when I'm Sad

A hand to Scold me when I'm Bad

Teaching me Right from Wrong

Telling me to Stand up and be Strong

And Sharing in my Happy Day

IN THE FAMILY WAY

Taking care of Each Other

Loving thy Sister and Brother

And sharing our Joys and Sorrows

Hoping for Better Tomorrows

Kneeling together to Pray

IN THE FAMILY WAY

We've been through so much together

But yet, we have Survived

We've had our share of Arguments and Fights

But yet, we are Alive

Through it all, we've Stuck together

Through Thick and Thin

And NO MATTER what Happens

Come what May

We'll be together

IN THE FAMILY WAY

You Believed in me

And I Trusted in you

Through and Through

We're one together on Earth to Stay

IN THE FAMILY WAY

We'll share our Love with other Kin

And Show them what

They've Been Missing

Gonna Live our Lives

From Day to Day

IN THE FAMILY WAY

BLAME IT ON THE MOON

FEELINGS RUN RAMPANT

THROUGH MORNING, NIGHT AND NOON

SO WHEN YOU GET THOSE FEELINGS

JUST BLAME IT ON THE MOON

BLAME IT ON THE MOON

When the Glow of Night is Shining Bright

And you just can't seem to Douse the Light

BLAME IT ON THE MOON

When you Start to Gaze

And Fall into a Haze

And find yourself Caught up in Amaze

BLAME IT ON THE MOON

When that Warm Sensation

Goes across your Chest

And you're feeling Kind of Anxious

And Just Can't Rest

And you just don't know what's Wrong

You feel a Need to go on a Quest

BLAME IT ON THE MOON

Feelings Run Rampant

Through Morning, Night and Noon

So when you get those Feelings

JUST BLAME IT ON THE MOON

MASK

Take off that MASK

That HIDES your Past

It's Ok to show the Real you

Like everyone else, we have made Mistakes

And are STRUGGLING Each Day

Just to Make it Through

Take a Deep Breath of Air

And Open up your Heart

If you CONTINUE TO HIDE your Feelings

You'll NEVER get a New Start

The Truth will Surface

And show up on your Face

So stop HIDING in the Bushes

And get Right Back in the Race

You have to look Towards the Future

And Let SOME THINGS Go

Get in Tuned with your Heart

And let your Feelings Flow

You'll Release some Pressure

And the Stress you will Relieve

So go on with your Life

And work Towards something to Achieve

Never LOSE SIGHT of Who You Are

Always know your SELF-WORTH

And know that you have Purpose

That's why you were Put Here on this Earth

TO OUR ANGELS

We know your Love Shines down on us

From Up Above

And Feel your Presence around us

Descending like a Dove

TO OUR ANGELS

To those that have Traveled

Into the Light

Looking down on us

With Smiles So Bright

You've done your Good Deeds

As REQUESTED from the Lord

And are now Resting in His Arms

And Receiving your Reward

Although we CAN NO LONGER see you

We FEEL you in our Heart

And the Warmth that we have Inside

Shall NEVER EVER Part

We know your Love Shines down on us

From Up Above

And Feel your Presence around us

Descending like a Dove

Although we MISS you

We know we WILL SEE

Your Face Again

Until then,

We say to you a GOOD FAREWELL

My Friend

A DREAM

Sometimes A DREAM is Good

And sometimes they are Bad

Sometimes A DREAM is Happy

But there are those that are Sad

Gwen Gibbs

A DREAM

A DREAM may seem Impossible

A DREAM may seem too Steep

A DREAM may seem unreachable

Just something you do in your Sleep

Sometimes A DREAM is Good

And sometimes they are Bad

Sometimes A DREAM is Happy

But there are those that are Sad

Some DREAMS

Are so Wonderful

You Wish they would NEVER END

But then,

Before you know it

Your Back to Reality Again

So DREAM on in your Sleep

And HOLD ON as long as you Can

Because with the Daylight you will Find

You've Drifted from Dreamland

DREAM SLEEP

I lay AWAKE in the Wee Hours

Of the Night

Can't get NO SLEEP

When you're Out of My Sight

I hear a Whisper in the Dark

Whenever we're apart

Could it REALLY be you

Or the Pounding of My Heart

Sometimes I see your Face

Up in the Cloud

You're Staring in my Face

And Laughing Out Loud

I feel a Love Tap upon my Shoulder

It looks like you're just

A Little Bit Older

I pick up the Phone to Make a Call

Then suddenly the Cord Rips

From the Wall

I Scream Out Loud

OH! WHAT COULD IT BE!

You answer in a Soft Brisk Voice MY SWEET

IT'S ONLY ME

No need to Fret or even Scream

The Truth of the Matter is

IT'S ONLY A DREAM

WHO ARE YOU?

Are you Sensitive

To the THINGS that people say

Allowing what's said to Determine

The OUTCOME of your Day

Letting others Push your Buttons

And take you there

Knowing that everyone's NOT Nice

And Life is just NOT Fair

Are you a People Pleaser

Trying to APPEASE everyone

Knowing that keeping everybody Happy

Just Can't Be Done

Being helpful Kind and Considerate

To keep the Peace AROUND

But knowing that somewhere someone's

Going to Try to Bring you Down

Are you a Hard-Working Person

That's trying to get a Break

Trying so hard to be Perfect

And Make NOT ONE MISTAKE

Beating yourself Over the Head

With each WRONG TURN you Take

Not Trusting in Yourself

And Wrestling with each Decision you Make

Are you that SELF-CENTERED PERSON

Who thinks the world Revolves around you

No one can Measure Up to your Standards

OR DO AS WELL AS YOU DO

Thinking everyone's Ideas are Bad

But yours are ALWAYS Good

If you keep up with that Mentality

You just might Fall where you Stood

Are you the Rational One in the Crowd

Who just Tries to make things Clear

You talk until you're Black and Blue

But very few have a Listening Ear

The fact is most people

Simply just want things to Go Their Way

And they will Stick to it

NO MATTER WHAT ANYONE HAS TO SAY

A MOTHER'S LOVE

A MOTHER'S LOVE

Can NEVER be Measured

It's something that just simply

Must Be Treasured

For who else can give us A MOTHER'S LOVE

As it is Meant to be Given

From the LORD Above

MOTHERS are sent from Heaven

To Nurture and Care

And be a Shoulder to Cry on

When we NEED them there

To Scold us when Needed

And give us an Occasional Whack

For sometimes that's what was needed

To get us Back on Track

For those whose Mothers are Gone

But with you in Heart

Remember ALL the Great Times you Spent

And NEVER let that Part

The Lessons and the Foundation they set

To Help us Grow

How much we Love and Appreciate them

WORDS CAN NEVER SHOW

So to all the Great Mothers out there who feel

UNAPPRECIATED

I understand because Motherhood

IS TRULY UNDERRATED

But be NOT DISCOURAGED

Because your Hard Work IS NOT IN VAIN

And with the day you will find your Sunshine

After the Rain

HELLO JANUARY

IN ALL OF ITS SPLENDOR

THE WINTER WINDS BLOW

IN A NIGHT TO REMEMBER

HELLO JANUARY

HELLO JANUARY

In ALL of its Splendor

The Winter Winds Blow

In a NIGHT to REMEMBER

Here's looking Towards the Future

And Leaving the Past Behind

Running Forward and Accomplishing

The things in my Mind

Building friendships from the Ground

Fixing Relationships

That were once Torn Down

Thinking of the Good things

And NOT the Bad

Focusing on the Happy Times

And NOT the Sad

Letting NO ONE Tear you Down

When times get Tough

STILL STAND YOUR GROUND

There are NEW EXPERIENCES

To look forward to

Strive to Reach your Goal

And be a Better you

So here's to JANUARY

In ALL of its Splendor

Why not make the Journey

One to Remember

Gwen Gibbs

SPRING FEVER

OH SPRING

OH SPRING

WE WELCOME THEE

BRING THE BEAUTIFUL FLOWING LEAVES

TO THE TREE

SPRING FEVER

The WARM SENSATION hits you

From the Beaming Sun

Which lets us know that SPRING

Has FINALLY Sprung

We look at the Branches

And see the Bubs appear

And we are convinced

That SPRING is Near

As the Grass turns Green

At the Light of Day

And the Kids are so Happy

To Go Out and Play

The Warmth by Day and Cool Breeze by Night

And with Anticipation we know

THAT SPRING'S IN SIGHT

OH SPRING

OH SPRING

We welcome thee

Bring the Beautiful Flowing Leaves

To the Tree

And make it known

That you are Near

Because SPRING FEVER

IS SURELY HERE

FREE

I want to be FREE like a Bird

Soaring through the Sky

FREE

Like the Plane that goes Flying by

FREE

Like a Ship Sailing on the Sea

FREE

To be WHATEVER I want to be

I want to be FREE as a Horse

Trotting through the City

FREE

As the Flowers that are Oh So Pretty

FREE

As the Sun that shines so Bright

FREE

As the Moon that Glows in the Night

To be FREE means a lot to me

So take it from me

SOMEDAY WE'LL ALL BE FREE

A POETS WORTH

Your body Fills with so much Emotion

That MUST Break Through

There's something seeded Deep Down

Inside of you

The Flurries you Feel

Once they start to Impart

That which speaks Volumes

Coming from your Heart

Those feelings Turn to Words

That you've Penned on your Paper

Now, as you Wipe Away the Sweat

That drips from your Upper Brow

The EXCITEMENT of it all seems to Spin

Your Head Around

As you Realize what's in you

MUST SURFACE AND NOT BE BOUND

To bring Life to what we Feel Passionate about

In the Depths of our Soul

And to Touch and Help someone along

This Journey called Life

IS A POET'S COMMON GOAL

IF ONLY

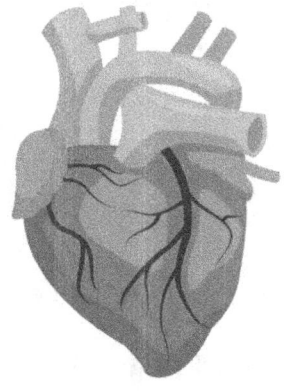

IF ONLY

You would have been there

I'd pour out my Heart but ONLY for you

IF ONLY

You'd act like you care

IF ONLY

IF ONLY

You knew what I've been going through

IF ONLY

You would have been there

I'd pour out my Heart but ONLY for you

IF ONLY

You'd act like you care

IF ONLY

You would ask How Was My Day?

And Greet me with a Nice Smile

You'd find that Good Things

MIGHT come your way

IF ONLY

You'd Show Love once in a while

IF ONLY

You would SOMETIMES be Kind

Instead of ALWAYS being So Cold

A Happier Life you just might find

Before you have come to be Too Old

IF ONLY

I knew then what I know now

Things surely would not be this way

I'd live my Life like I know how

Instead of Dry, Gloomy, and Grey

ANGELS WATCHING OVER ME

I've got ANGELS WATCHING OVER ME

Wherever I Look is where they'll be

To keep me out of Harms Way

And Safely Guide me THROUGH My Day

To Whisper in my Ear when I CAN'T See

And Lead me AWAY from Misery

I've got ANGELS WATCHING OVER ME

To Help me up if I should Fall

To Push Me Over that Scaling Wall

To remind me that

I am a Child of the Most High God

And to Stand out and Be Set Apart

Even though it makes me Feel Odd

I've got ANGELS WATCHING OVER ME

To show me what is Right and Wrong

And when I am Weak

God will make me Strong

To Comfort me when I Grieve

And let me know that

I MUST Believe

To give me a Shake

When I'm out of Whack

And into the Father's Good Graces

THEY LEAD ME BACK

Our ANGELS are around us

By Night and by Day

To keep our Mind Stayed on Jesus

And KEEP Satan away

To Divert the Hand of the enemy

While on this Earth

For Jesus is the VICTOR

Who gives us ALL NEW BIRTH

The Lord will keep His Hand upon us

As long as we Obey

But if by chance He should see fit

He'll let us GO ASTRAY

No sooner than He Turns us Loose

We'll reach out for His Hand

Because WITHOUT Jesus in our Lives

NO ONE COULD EVER STAND

For out in the Wilderness

We may Roam for A While

But when we Return to Jesus

HE'LL SAY WELCOME BACK MY CHILD

BE NOT DECEIVED

Some Green

Some Blue

Saying, how do you do

Some you Sniff

Some you Swallow

Some you Puff from a Bottle

Some are Big

Some are Small

Some make you Feel

TEN FEET TALL

Some bring you Up

Some take you Down

Some have your Head

SPINNING AROUND

Feeling Good got that Hit

And Believing at Any Time

YOU CAN QUIT

But you Come Down from that High

And with Life you CANNOT Cope

So you run out to the Nearest Corner

Looking to Score some more Dope

Thought you had it All Together

Thought you could Handle it

But when you are Without it

You throw a Real Hissy Fit

Its Presence is Overwhelming

When it gets you in its Grip

And if you are not Careful

Your Life will become a Long Drawn Out Trip

ABOUT THE AUTHOR

My name is Gwen Gibbs, I am married with two daughters. I am the second youngest out of my seven siblings.

I have always had a passion for writing. I started writing at the age of 12 and find it so fulfilling to share the voice that stirs my soul with others.

It is truly a blessing that God has equipped me with this gift. And I carry it proudly and take it not for granted. I am the author of another Book of Poetry titled: Guided by Grace which was published in 2009.

Guided by Grace - A Book of Poetry

Published in 2009

REFERENCES FOR THE IMAGES

www.thecitynotforsaken.com, istockphotos, fitlife.tv, discipleblog, www.brusheezy.com, askideas, fssba.org, www.wallpapersite.com, www.irishcentral.com full-moon-name, www.pintrest.com, www.prevuemeetings.com, YouTube, www.heartlandshome.com/entry-doors/joyce-meyers; virgorising101.wordpress.com, isallygraves.wordpress www.sermonview.com/LatterRain.main.jpg,theenchantedmanor.com, https://wordpress.com/do-not-grieve-the-holy-spirit- https://health.sunnybrook.ca, https://clipartstation.com, https://www.futurescommunitysupport.com, https://www.futurescommunitysupport.comjanuary-newsletter, https://www.npr.org/black-santa-claus-is-a-hit-in-the-mall-but-faces-an-online-backlash/

www.ingramcontent.com/pod-product-compliance
Lightning Source LLC
Chambersburg PA
CBHW070900080526
44589CB00013B/1141